G000021634

SUSSEX in photographs

SUSSEX in photographs

photographs by Anthony Kersting
text by Judith Glover

B. T. BATSFORD LTD, LONDON

title page Brighton's Royal Pavilion, one of the country's most idiosyncratic buildings, built at the beginning of the 19th century for the Prince Regent

First published 1976

ISBN 0 7134 3197 0

Printed in Great Britain by
Butler & Tanner Ltd. Frome, Somerset
Filmset by Keyspools Limited, Golborne, Lancashire

for the Publishers B. T. Batsford Limited
4 Fitzhardinge Street, London W1H 0AH

Contents

Introduction

In the unlikely event of this island sinking beneath the waves, leaving only Sussex undrowned, England's heritage and most that is best in the national character would surely remain as well represented to the world as it has always been.

For this is the most English of counties; a county for all seasons, all pursuits and all pleasures, offering a most enviable range of diversities whether the interest is active or passive, visual or mental, extrovert or introspective. No guest or visitor need search too far or too wide to find his preferred reward in this county which is so rich in the good, honest loam of English history and tradition.

Sussex's very appearance offers many contrasts. Unlike its level coastal belt and the hills of the Downland country, its Weald is a smooth basin of agricultural land lying behind the bastion of the South Downs, a rolling plain dotted about with hursts and spinneys, while to the north rises the Ashdown Forest, which – together with those other Sussex 'forests' of Balcombe, Worth, Holmbush, Tilgate, Peasepottage and St Leonard's – is the last remnant of the immense Saxon *Andredesweald* which once clothed the entire plain with a thick, dense covering of oak; oak so plenteous that it was still known until comparatively recent times as 'Sussex weed'. Ashdown is no longer a forest: its trees are scattered into woods and the lovely heathland which it has now become is broken by roads and villages.

Yet it is still remote in parts, the delight of the weekend walker and the naturalist: a complete contrast to the coastal level beyond the great Downs, busy with its round-the-year seaside towns which, though all catering for their visitors and trade, are each in their own way quite different from the others. Brighton, for instance, with its fantastic Pavilion, classical architecture and famous antiques quarter, The Lanes, is not at all like Hastings, a town which in itself is divided between sedate residential areas, holiday makers' amusement arcades and fun parks for family entertainment, and its Old Town, a more serene relic of tradition and unchange with its high Norman castle and long established fishing fleet. Different again is Eastbourne, pleasantly refined, from Worthing, say, or Bognor Regis, the one modest and relaxed, the other with its holiday camps and bustling activity.

Inland the contrast is everywhere, too. There are towns like Rye, haunt of the artist and writer, with narrow cobbled streets and a jumbled mosaic of old houses, cottages and inns leaning in their old-time beauty above the heads of visitors; and towns like Haywards Heath or Crawley, thoroughly modern and practical, and yet quite as necessary to the welfare of Sussex as its more quaintly beautiful settlements. And there is Chichester, quite unique, the county's only cathedral city, displaying the best of both old and new and proud of its fine heritage and its cultural and commercial strength.

There are interesting differences to be noted between villages like West Burton, Amberley and Fittleworth, replete with their quota of neat thatched cottages with gingham curtains, a pot of red geraniums and a cat in the window, and villages whose pride is in their overlordship of stately homes, in particular those of Petworth, Uppark and Parham. Sturdy communities have grown through the centuries around the great religious establishments which include the priories of Boxgrove and Michelham, and Battle Abbey; and around the even more historic churches such as Sussex's three 'Saxon treasures': Sompting, Alfriston and Worth. Towns have sprung up in the shadow of the county's impressive and evocative castles of Arundel, Lewes, Herstmonceux and Bodiam; while the ghosts of towns long dead have their monument in such proud Roman remains as those to be found at Bignor, Old Fishbourne and Pevensey. There is always something to arrest the eye and absorb the mind. Many Sussex windmills are still in use, and those which aren't are mostly picturesque. The beautiful gardens and parks, such as Sheffield Park, Nymans near Handcross, and Wakehurst Place, are visited from all parts of the world for their attractiveness as much as from interest in the species they contain. The range of man-made architecture, whether it be the small old houses saved from destruction at the Open Air Museum at Singleton, the imposing facade of Lancing College, or that strange Sugar Loaf folly on Brightling Down, is great; while Nature's own architecture has no more breath-taking views to display than those from such vantage points as Beachy Head, Devil's Dyke or Chanctonbury, or pleasanter sights than in the vicinity of the county's five principal rivers.

Sussex can offer, too, the best to those who like to participate as well as to stand and admire. There is racing at Goodwood, cricket at The Saffrons and elsewhere, tennis tournaments at Devonshire Park in Eastbourne, international chess at Hastings, yachting and water sports at Bosham – and soon at Brighton's great new marina – polo at Cowdray Park, hang-gliding at Steyning Bowl; and golf, football, swimming, fishing and horse riding, and many long and rewarding walks to be enjoyed on the smooth green expanses of the South Downs. Some of the world's best opera performances are given at Glyndebourne, near Lewes; and Chichester's is only one of the many fine theatres, while there are concert halls, museums and galleries throughout the county.

Apart from a few of the major arterial roads running south to the coast, and the A272 slanting laterally across the county into Hampshire, the roads of Sussex are mercifully uncluttered with commercial traffic and offer pleasant and varied motoring. The towns and villages are definite and apart, separate entities, so that between them there is wide green country to be enjoyed along the uninterrupted miles of good rural roads. For those who care to venture off the well-mapped route, there are side turnings, pointed to by wooden signposts with intriguing names such as Fivemile Ash, Little Trodgers and Harebeating. These are the true English lanes, winding easily past woods and high hedges towards their destination, and once there, curving away into a sudden turn to other happy discoveries.

Not all that long ago in terms of the history of this very old county – in 1771 to be precise – John Burton was commenting on the national notoriety of these by-ways: 'Why is it that the oxen, the swine, the women, and all other animals, are so long-legged in Sussex?' he asked. 'May it be from the difficulty of pulling the feet out of so much mud by the strength of the ankles that the muscles get stretched, as it were, and the bones lengthened?'

He was referring to the 'slubby' or sticky texture of the Wealden clay which often caused travellers to sink deep into the mire of the ways. One old Sussex tale – tongue in cheek, maybe – tells of a farmer standing disconsolately up to his hams in a mud-drowned lane. When questioned why he stayed there he said that his haywain and team of horses had sunk beneath him into the mire, and all were waiting to be extricated to continue their journey.

Thankfully, those uneasy days of travel are past, and the visitor to Sussex will find his path a smooth and pleasant one.

It is difficult to plan how best to present this varied and beautiful county in order to do full justice to it in a little under two hundred photographs: from any viewpoint its typical Englishness is apparent in the many cameos of natural setting or of man-made presentation. But the administrative county division between east and west, and the long slash of the A272 between north and south have eased my task. On the whole, the division into four quarters is easily achieved, and this has been my guiding pattern, underlining the divergent character of Sussex.

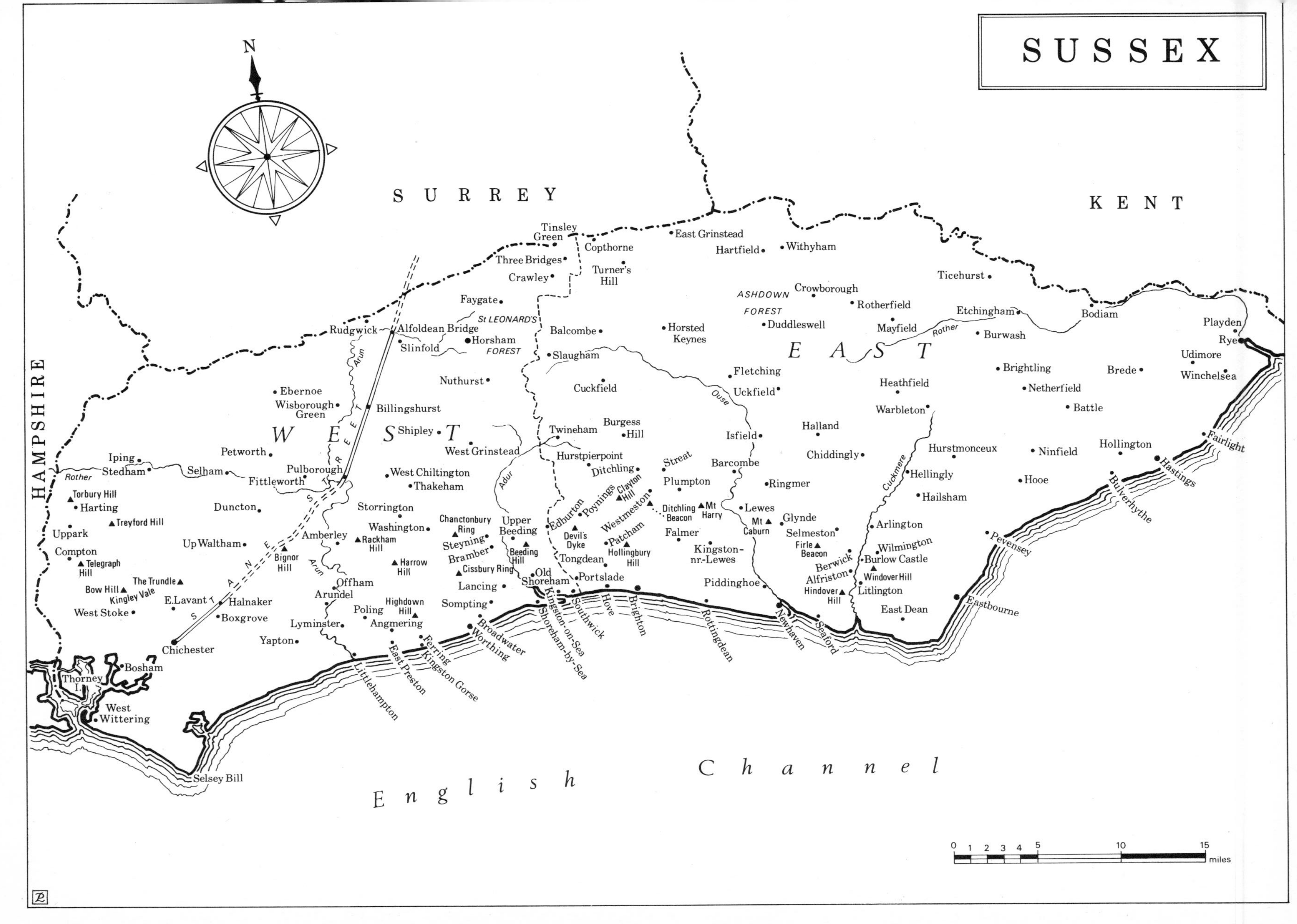

SUSSEX
N
SURREY
KENT
HAMPSHIRE
WEST
EAST
English Channel
Tinsley Green
Copthorne
East Grinstead
Hartfield
Withyham
Three Bridges
Crawley
Turner's Hill
Ticehurst
Faygate
ASHDOWN FOREST
Crowborough
Rotherfield
Etchingham
Bodiam
Playden
Rye
Rudgwick
Alfoldean Bridge
St LEONARD'S FOREST
Horsham
Slinfold
Balcombe
Horsted Keynes
Duddleswell
Mayfield
Rother
Burwash
Udimore
Winchelsea
Slaughham
Fletching
Brightling
Brede
Ebernoe
Wisborough Green
Nuthurst
Cuckfield
Uckfield
Heathfield
Netherfield
Battle
Billingshurst
Ouse
Warbleton
Arun
Shipley
Twineham
Burgess Hill
Isfield
Halland
Fairlight
Hollington
Iping
Petworth
West Grinstead
Hurstpierpoint
Streat
Barcombe
Chiddingly
Hurstmonceux
Ninfield
Hastings
Stedham
Rother
Selham
Pulborough
Fittleworth
STANE STREET
West Chiltington
Thakeham
Ditchling
Plumpton
Ringmer
Hellingly
Cuckmere
Hooe
Bulverhythe
Torbury Hill
Harting
Duncton
Storrington
Adur
Poynings
Clayton Hill
Westmeston
Ditchling Beacon
Mt Harry
Lewes
Hailsham
Treyford Hill
Washington
Chanctonbury Ring
Upper Beeding
Edburton
Devil's Dyke
Patcham
Falmer
Mt Caburn
Glynde
Arlington
Uppark
Up Waltham
Amberley
Rackham Hill
Steyning
Bramber
Beeding Hill
Hollingbury Hill
Selmeston
Pevensey
Compton
Telegraph Hill
Bignor Hill
Harrow Hill
Cissbury Ring
Tongdean
Kingston-nr.-Lewes
Firle Beacon
Wilmington
Burlow Castle
Berwick
Alfriston
Windover Hill
The Trundle
Bow Hill
Kingley Vale
E.Lavant
Halnaker
Offham
Arundel
Lancing
Old Shoreham
Portslade
Piddinghoe
Hindover Hill
Litlington
East Dean
West Stoke
Boxgrove
Highdown Hill
Sompting
Eastbourne
Chichester
Lyminster
Poling
Angmering
Yapton
Broadwater
Worthing
Kingston-on-Sea
Shoreham-by-Sea
Southwick
Hove
Brighton
Rottingdean
Newhaven
Seaford
Bosham
Thorney I.
West Wittering
Ferring
Kingston Gorse
East Preston
Littlehampton
Selsey Bill
0 1 2 3 4 5 10 15 miles

left The Ashdown Forest at Wych Cross, where 15 acres of National Trust woodland mark its western limit.

top right Cuckfield Park, an Elizabethan manor house close to Cuckfield village.

right The handsome brick gatehouse with mullioned windows.

Bayham Abbey, near Wadhurst, described as 'the most impressive monastic ruin of Sussex', seen from the south-east.

The transept of the 13th century abbey, a Premonstratensian house dissolved during the Reformation.

The view from the ruins of new Bayham Abbey, a mock-Tudor mansion standing across the county border in Kent.

Sackville College at East Grinstead, bequeathed in 1617 by Robert Sackville, 2nd Earl of Dorset.

A view across the lake of the much-visited gardens at Sheffield Park, near Fletching.

Rudyard Kipling's home, Bateman's, in the village of Burwash. The house is now National Trust property and open to the public.

The gardens at Bateman's were largely created by Kipling himself.

left The Sugar Loaf Folly on Brightling Down, built by the early 19th century politician 'Mad Jack' Fuller in order to win a wager.

right A view over Brightling Down towards the Needle obelisk.

right Looking southward over the Sussex Weald from the Needle.

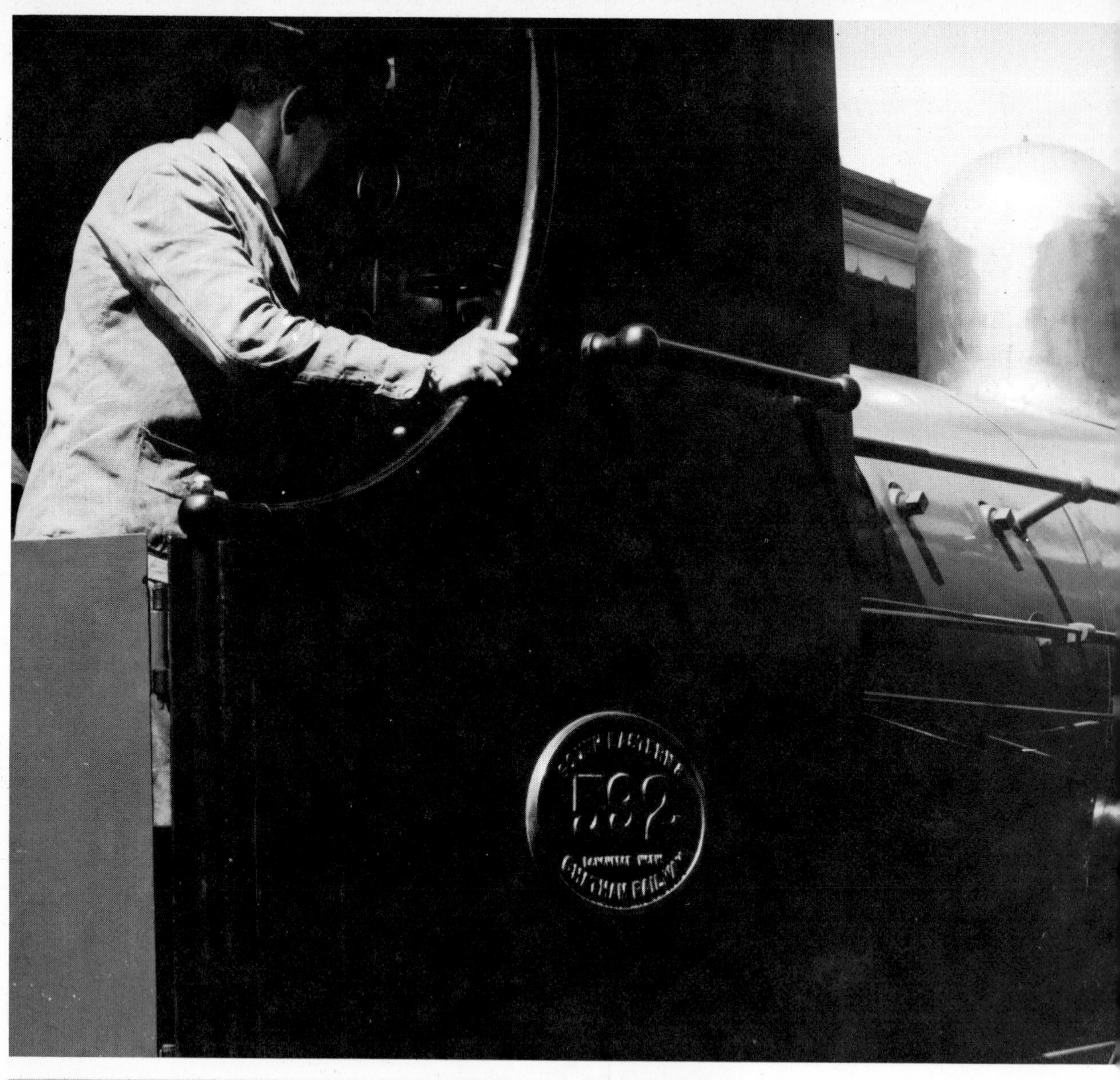

A reminder of the great age of steam on the Bluebell Railway line, running between Horsted Keynes and Sheffield Park.

The northern terminal of the Bluebell Railway, some way outside the village of Horsted Keynes.

One of the finest post mills in the south of England is this one at Argos Hill, near Mayfield.

Mayfield's main street with its village sign below the church spire.

The 15th century gatehouse of the Convent of the Holy Child Jesus in Mayfield.

he Chapel of Mayfield Convent: the uilding comprises the remains of a alace of the Archbishops of anterbury.

narled beeches in Worth Forest, a emnant of ancient *Andredesweald*.

Great Dixter, near Northiam. The manor house, dating from the mid-15th century, was restored in 1910 by Sir Edward Lutyens.

left The hall of Great Dixter with its splendid roof of hammer and tie beams.

right The sunken garden in the grounds of Great Dixter, which attract many visitors throughout the year.

ne of the three Saxon treasures of
ssex is Worth Church, seen here from
e east.

he nave of Worth Church with its
axon chancel arch.

The 13th century stone font at Worth.

The walls of medieval Bodiam Castle, mirrored in the waters of its moat-lake.

The Hay Waggon Inn at Hartfield.

Autumnal landscape in the Ashdown Forest – now more heathland than true forest.

Ardingly College seen from the lake in the grounds.

The courtyard, showing the chapel of the College, founded in 1858.

Wakehurst Place near Ardingly. Only the wings remain of this late Elizabethan house.

ɟt The lily pond in the grounds of
ɅVakehurst Place, which are leased by
ɪe National Trust as an addition to the
ɔyal Botanic Gardens at Kew.

Gravetye Manor, near West Hoathly, an Elizabethan iron master's home.

ɔottom left The Westwood Valley lake
ɿ the grounds.

The railway viaduct at Balcombe, carrying the line to Brighton across the Ouse valley.

The Limeburners Arms at Newbridge.

A winter setting for the early 17th century Manor House at West Hoathly.

above Rye harbour, used both by pleasure craft and by the fishing fleet which reaches the sea by way of the River Rother here.

Lamb House seen at the foot of West Street in Rye. For many years it was the home of the American novelist Henry James.

Rye's 18th century Town Hall with the Norman church of St. Mary behind.

left Timber-framed houses on the west side of the churchyard.

One of Rye's greatest attractions, cobbled Mermaid Street leads down to the Strand.

below Old warehouses on the Strand beside the River Tillingham.

ar left All that remains of the early Norman castle at Bramber are fragments of the massive walls.

eft The popular seaside resort of Saltdean.

left The pond in the village of Rottingdean with Rudyard Kipling's house beyond. He lived here 1897–1902 before moving to Bateman's at Burwash.

top Kipling's neighbour, the artist Sir Edward Burne-Jones, lived at this house in Rottingdean for the last 20 years of his life.

above The Long Man of Wilmington, a chalk figure 240 feet high on the side of Windover Hill. It is the only such carving on the Sussex Downs.

left Lewes, county town of East Sussex, with the Downs on the horizon.

right The barbican, or outer gatehouse, of Lewes Castle.

far right Keere Street, a typical Sussex 'twitten', or steep alley. The Prince Regent is said to have driven a coach-and-four at full gallop down the slope.

left Looking down Lewes High Street towards The Cliffe.

left Anne of Cleves House, now the folk museum of the Sussex Archaeological Society.

right Shelleys Hotel in Lewes High Street: a Georgian frontage conceals an Elizabethan inn.

SHELLEYS HOTEL

The handsome wooden smock mill at Chailey.

Blossom in the National Trust gardens at Nymans, near Handcross.

The tie beam and queenpost roof inside the enormous Barn of Michelham Priory near Hailsham, founded in 1229 for Augustinian Canons.

below The house at Nymans, destroyed by fire in 1947 and now a romantic ruin.

ft Winchelsea church: only the
ıancel and side chapels remain of the
iginal early medieval building.

ght One of the county's best loved
sorts is Eastbourne with its fine prom-
ıade and pier and many amenities.

ght The famous Carpet Gardens
ong the three-mile seafront.

ft The tomb of Gervase de Alard, first
dmiral of the Cinque Ports, in the south
isle of Winchelsea church.

ight Eastbourne's famous Wish
ower, a Martello Tower built to defend
his part of the coast during the Napo-
eonic Wars.

The Norman church at Friston seen from its Sussex 'tapsell' gate.

right Pevensey Castle ruins enclosed by the Roman walls of the ancient fort of *Anderida*.

One of the narrow stairways leading to the basement of the keep, built when the castle was used by the Home Guard during the Second World War.

right Beachy Head, almost 600 feet high, the eastern termination of the South Downs.

left Pevensey village high street from the castle gateway.

below Castle and church seen from the banks of Pevensey Haven.

The De La Warr Pavilion on the front at Bexhill-on-Sea.

The village of Telscombe lying in a hollow in the South Downs.

Telscombe's small Norman flint church, focus of the village.

above The chinoiserie decorations of the Music Salon of the Brighton Royal Pavilion.

The entrance to The Lanes, Brighton's antiques quarter.

Part of the four-mile long seafront at Brighton.

below Royal Crescent, facing the sea, built between 1798–1807.

ussex Square, in Brighton's Kemp Town istrict, belongs to the early 19th century.

elow The village pond at Falmer, a retty village close to the University of ussex.

Looking westward over the South Downs near Clayton, with Chanctonbury Ring on the skyline.

r left 'Jack', a smock mill, one of the air of mills on Clayton Hill.

ft His partner 'Jill', a post mill.

ottom left Together they are one of he most attractive sights in the county.

ght The Victorian Gothic railway tun-el entrance at Clayton.

elow Herstmonceux Castle, dating rom the mid-15th century, now the ome of the Royal Observatory.

The Seven Sisters, one of the glories of the Sussex coast, seen from the coast-guard cottages at Seaford Head.

The Star Inn at Alfriston, once the headquarters of the notorious Alfriston smuggling gang.

below Alfriston church, known as 'The Cathedral of the Downs'.

above The unique net drying sheds in Hastings Old Town. Behind them is the Fishermen's Chapel of St. Nicholas.

The ruins of Hastings Castle, high on its hill above the town.

eft Hastings Old Town.

ght Panorama of Downs and Weald, ooking northward from Devil's Dyke bove Brighton.

ight Brunswick Terrace, a fine example of Regency architecture at Hove.

left Fishing boats on the beach below The Stade in Hastings.

right Anne of Cleves House at Ditchling.

Battle Abbey, dominating its town, built by William the Conqueror soon after the Battle of Hastings.

The undercroft of the dorter within the Norman abbey.

The ruins of Camber Castle, built during the reign of Henry VIII to protect the coastline against attack by the French.

The Saxon church at Bishopstone, near the mouth of the River Ouse.

The beach at Birling Gap, a natural cleft in the chalk face of the South Downs.

above The Victorian bandstand on the Carfax at the centre of Horsham.

Old houses bordering Horsham Causeway.

above right The Grinling Gibbons Room at Petworth House created by the master carver in 1692.

above A detail of the intricate carving worked by Gibbons.

right The Grand Staircase with wall paintings by Louis Laguerre, c.1720.

top left The 15th century bridge spanning the Arun at Stopham.

left Looking across the deer park towards the west front of Petworth House, dominating the town of that name.

above Inside the late 17th century chapel at Petworth House.

left The windmill at Shipley, a wooden galleried smock mill closely associated with Hilaire Belloc, who lived at King's Land beside it.

opposite top left The upper reaches of the River Adur with Shipley mill in the background.

opposite top right Pulborough's early 15th century church of St Mary, and the War Memorial.

right The Plough Inn at Redford, near Midhurst.

above Looking towards the South Downs from Blackdown, the highest point in Sussex.

The Elizabethan monument to the 1st Viscount Montague in Easebourne church.

sunlit clearing in The Mens Wood, ear Petworth, which belongs to the ussex Trust for Nature Conservation.

Crimbourne Farm, near Petworth, one of he many attractive old buildings of Sussex.

The courtyard of Cowdray House at Midhurst: the building was destroyed by fire in 1793, traditionally as part of the fulfillment of the Cowdray Curse.

below Cowdray's old half-timbered Granary supported on staddlestones stands within the courtyard.

bove Looking across the polo ground
ı Cowdray Park towards the South
owns.

ight The attractive old town of Mid-
urst seen from the banks of its lake.

ight The 16th century Angel Hotel in
Aidhurst's main street: the Pilgrim Fath-
ers are said to have stayed here on their
vay to embark in the *Mayflower*.

Tile-hung and half-timbered cottages in Wool Lane, Midhurst.

below Cricket on the village green at Lurgashall, below the slopes of Blackdown.

Castle Goring, near Goring-on-Sea, a bizarre mixture of architectural styles.

above Chanctonbury, the best-known of the Sussex landmarks, crowned by its grove of beech trees.

The view from Chanctonbury, high on the South Downs.

he chancel of Boxgrove Priory Church, aid to be the second finest example of arly English building in Sussex.

The De La Warr chantry within the church, the only complete chantry chapel in the county.

right The soaring spire of Chichester Cathedral, seen from the south-east.

left The nave of the cathedral showing the gallery and transverse arches of the Norman building.

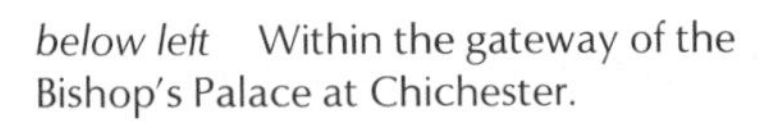

below left Within the gateway of the Bishop's Palace at Chichester.

below The Head of Christ in one of the cathedral's Romanesque panels, depicting the Raising of Lazarus from the Dead.

St Mary's Hospital in the cathedral precincts, founded in 1158 as a hospice, or Maison Dieu.

The entrance to St Mary's Hospital.

The Roman palace at Old Fishbourne on the western edge of Chichester, built about AD 75.

above One of the magnificent mosaic pavements inside the palace.

The box hedges at Old Fishbourne follow the original Roman garden design.

Pallant House, in Chichester's North Pallant, is also called Dodo House from the stone birds on the gateposts.

The interior of St John's Church in Chichester, showing the gallery and 'three-decker' pulpit.

Fifteenth century houses in Vicars Close in the precincts, overlooked by the cathedral spire.

he medieval Market Cross at the
entre of Chichester.

elow The Chichester Festival Theatre
n Oaklands Park, opened in 1962.

eft Ox-bows forming in the river ·alley as the Cuckmere winds its way to he sea at Cuckmere Haven.

ight The inner courtyard of Parham, he Tudor manor house close to \mberley, open to the public for much of the year.

The Great Hall, showing the windows of the steward's room high on the right.

left Winter scene with the little church of St Mary the Virgin at Upwaltham.

The famous Long Gallery at the top of the house at Parham.

Looking towards Arundel and its castle from the banks of the Arun.

right The massive walls of Arundel Castle, home of the Dukes of Norfolk, hereditary Earls Marshall of England.

below The interior of the Fitzalan Chapel in the castle grounds, dating from 1380.

Tomb of the 5th Earl of Arundel (*d.* 1415) and his wife in the Fitzalan Chapel at Arundel Castle.

Hiorn's Tower, standing in the castle park, built in 1790.

Looking from Findon towards Cissbury Ring on the South Downs.

Bosham harbour, well known to water sports enthusiasts, with the Saxon church in the background.

Winter landscape on the South Downs near Findon.

Uppark, the Wren-style house high on the Downs near South Harting.

below The Red Drawing Room at Uppark showing part of the Rococo ceiling and the original wallpaper and mirrors.

The curtain wall of 14th century Amberley Castle, once the property of the Bishops of Chichester.

below Amberley Castle seen from the water meadows bordering the Arun.

above St Michael's unusual sermon glass in its iron bracket beside the pulpit.

left The Norman church of St Michael at Amberley, showing the carved chancel arch and one of the medieval wall paintings.

below Goodwood House, close to the famous racecourse to which it has given its name.

The south front of Goodwood House.

left The famous 'Rhenish helm' tower of Sompting Church, one of the three Saxon treasures of Sussex.

below left Detail of a Saxon carved stone inside the church.

below The trefoil-headed piscina in the north wall of the nave.

above The Red Lion Inn at Old Shoreham.

right The chequerboard front of the Marlipins Museum in New Shoreham, believed to have been a medieval Customs House.

below Low tide in Shoreham harbour.

left Looking towards the county's best-known landmark, Chanctonbury Ring, from Warren Hill near Washington.

above William Blake, the great poet and artist, lived at this cottage in Blake's Road, Felpham, between 1800 and 1803.

below An austere setting for Lancing College Chapel beside the River Adur.

e Weald and Downland Open Air
useum outside Singleton, showing a
alden timber-framed farmhouse.

elow West Dean Park, near Chiches-
er, a Georgian 'Gothick' house of 1804.

Index